Love Your Neighbor

Love
Your Neighbor

Louis Evely

Translated by
Imelda L'Italien, P.M.

HERDER AND HERDER

1969
HERDER AND HERDER NEW YORK
232 Madison Avenue, New York, N.Y. 10016

Original edition:
L'Eglise et les sacrements,
published by the author.

Nihil obstat: Leo J. Steady, Censor Librorum
Imprimatur: ✠Robert F. Joyce, Bishop of Burlington
March 11, 1969

Contents

1.

The Epiphany

The feast of the Epiphany celebrates God's manifestation. The essential element of the Christian religion is that God reveals himself to man, that God comes to us, and that he makes himself known to us at our level, the measure of man. The essential factor of Christianity is that we know God in a sensible form.

To begin with, this summary surprises us. We are much more accustomed to say that God exacts faith, obscurity, and obedience. Yet, it is perfectly true to say that God is light, revelation, and Epiphany. That which differentiates the Christian religion from any other is that it is a religion of incarnation, a sacramental religion where God reveals himself and always has revealed himself to our senses.

Already, the creation of man to the image and resemblance of God pointed towards this plan, this possible communication between him and us. "When he formed Adam's body," the Fathers of the Church tell us, "God already thought of Christ who would become man some day." Man was created to be permeated by God. Ever since the Garden of Eden, God was Epiphany; he came with the night breeze to talk familiarly to Adam. God heard himself; he communicated with man in a human way. He confided in him. Thus Adam entered into God's confidence. God gives himself to man, and in so doing, he betrays himself. God's passion, where he revealed that he was vulnerable to an audacious and rash love, began in the garden of paradise.

Adam rejected this revelation, and he became darkness. Sin is the state where God is unknown and unfelt. We are all familiar with this condition. Darkness does not capture God; furthermore it refuses to grasp him.

However, God did not get discouraged. He did not cease to communicate himself. He revealed himself; he raised the dark veil which had dropped between him and us. He called Abraham, and Abraham heard him. Abraham had the joy of hearing him with his ears, of seeing him with his eyes, of receiving him in his tent, and of assisting at God's Epiphany in the most incredible birth, the most dolorous paternal sacrifice. God revealed himself to Moses in a burning bush on smoky Sinai. God spoke to Moses face to face, as a man speaks to his friend. He spoke through the prophets; each of them was seized, drawn out of himself and invaded by this most familiar, yet overwhelming presence. The pillar of clouds or of fire, the Tabernacle, and the Temple were God's first incarnations, the first testimonies to our eyes and to our hands that God walks with us: Emmanuel.

With time, the veil was raised even higher until the coming of Jesus. It was eventually torn from top to bottom. "I am with you all days, even unto the consummation of the world" (Matthew 28, 20). "The Epiphany and the Incarnation are constant exigencies of Christian life," says Romano Guardini. The sacraments are visible signs because there was an Incarnation and because there is an Epiphany.

God decided to reach us where we are. St. John's astonishment: "What we have heard, what we have seen with our eyes, what we have looked upon and our hands have handled: of the Word of Life. And the Life was made known and we have

12

seen . . ." (1 John 1, 1), expresses the rapture of a permanent Epiphany to which God invites us in communion through the sacraments.

Blessed are the pure of heart for they see God. The normal state, the human condition is to see God, to perceive him in the tangible, the ordinary, and the familiar. God is with us forever. The liturgy is God's Epiphany for each of us who participates with an open heart, The Word dwells with us, and we see his glory. A real Mass, a beautiful celebration of the sacraments or of prayer, is God's manifestation through visible signs.

When the Church solemnly proclaims the Gospel at Mass, we answer, "Glory to you, Lord." Upon hearing the Gospel, how often have you benefited from an Epiphany? How often have you seen the glory of God?

What I mean is this: when Jesus spoke, two attitudes, which still exist today, were possible.

Obdurate hearts heard the word of God, but they were indifferent spectators, impervious to grace and reticent. When he had finished his sermon, they had retained nothing except, perhaps, an objection or a criticism. What do you get out of reading the Gospel or hearing a homily that explains it? If someone asked us, as we come out of church, how much we have retained of what we have heard, how confused we would be to admit that we remember nothing. And yet, there has been an Epiphany of God, "He who hears you, hears me" (Luke 10, 16).

When Jesus taught, the pure of heart let themselves be instructed, formed, and transformed by his word. Theirs was a favorable reaction. His word revealed to them who God was and who they were; how God treated them and how they treated

13

God. They discovered God's plan, their resistance, his call. An indescribable emotion stirred the creature at the approach of his Creator. His sheep heard his voice, and they followed him. Those who belonged to the fold were filled with delight when they heard the word of God resound. They felt an awakening of the innermost parts of their beings. Their hearts glowed while he spoke to them. Immense outbursts of faith, love, and confusion, both infinite and sweet, swelled forth from their beings. They were stirred, drawn to him, oftentimes without knowing why. When they returned home disturbed, changed, sorrowful but serene, others queried, "What did he say? What proof has he given? What is so extraordinary about him?" They were unable to answer, so they kept quiet in order better to remember, to relive the happy moments when he had transported them. They were content to say, "Never has a man spoken as this man" (John 7, 46).

They had seen his glory because their hearts were pure. Holy Mass is God's Epiphany, not for those who are merely present in body, but for those who get involved. When Christ was born, the Palestinians knew what had to be known; yet, they did not see him. The Magi saw him; they knew infinitely less, but seeing a mysterious light, they *believed* it was meant for them. They had *faith;* they left heartily. They *came;* they participated actively in the liturgy of the Incarnation. They communicated to this joy. They answered the call, made their offering, adored, and they saw him.

From time to time, in someone, in a ceremony, in a reunion, we have felt that God was there. He was suddenly present among us, visible and felt. Darkness was dissipated, and we saw what

14

his glory was. Intervals of light are, without doubt, intercepted by so much darkness. But if there was light once, this is sufficient to know that light always exists and to believe in the Epiphany, regardless of the impurity of our own hearts.

2.

Sacraments

The Church teaches with truth, but if she only taught, she would perhaps be an instructor, a preacher, or a doctor. She would not be a mother.

The Church is a mother because she does more than just talk; she procreates, she generates life, a new life called "grace," because it is given more gratuitously, more generously, and more abundantly than ordinary life. The life of grace makes us children of the Church, and since we have received it from the same mother, it should make us all brothers and sisters.

It is this life that the Church speaks of with authority, as a mother explains or should make clear to her children the wonder of their birth and the rules of health. Church dogmas are not intellectual obstacles that make our way to salvation more meritorious. They are the rational expression of a life that infinitely transcends them.

Christ is the first who lived this life, and all Christian life is but the participation of the actual manifestation of his life. This grace of Christ is communicable; divine life, the life of love, is transmittable. You can begin to love with a love that you have never known before, a love which is not yours; nevertheless, it alone is capable of answering the needs of those who surround you, and it can enrich your own poor heart.

In each of us, Christ is seeking a new incarnation; Christ begs of every one of us a prolongation of his humanity so that he may relive this human life that he loved so much, in which he delighted, in which he honored his Father so well, comforted the afflicted, and reconciled sinners.

Christ's incarnation in a particular human nature only served to merit and reveal a permanent incarnation in the entire humanity. All men were incorporated in his life. In thirty-three years, Christ was incapable of manifesting all the love of God that animated him. He could only live one life; he could only die one death. However, there was in him a love that was capable of transcending all love and accepting all deaths. Each man who lends himself to him completes in his body what is lacking to the passion of Christ. He gives Christ the very stuff of incarnation, that which enables Him to live, to suffer, and to die anew. What Christ desires is to incarnate himself, especially in your life, something you generally do not want. He desires to take possession of this banal, empty life which he alone can fill to the brim with love and ennoble it. To live your life simply demands nothing less than all of God's love.

This communion to Christ, this new incarnation becomes possible in and by the sacraments. A sacrament is a gesture of Christ, a place where he begins to exist anew and to act for all those who are united to him in faith. A sacrament is a means of suppressing time and making Christ present in our midst today as he lived in Palestine, and as he will return at the end of time. Each sacrament has three dimensions: the past, the present, and the future. It is a past event that becomes present again and foreshadows a coming occurrence. "For as often as you shall eat this bread and drink the cup, you proclaim the death of the Lord, until he comes" (1 Corinthians 11, 26).

20

The Church is the setting of Christ's permanent incarnation. Christ has neither successor nor substitute, nor representative. He has a real living body that he animates by his own principle. Too often we consider our religion sentimentally. "If we had seen Christ, if He had spoken to us, if we had lived during His time." Little do we realize that the sacraments are a prolongation of Christ's body so that we may see him, hear him, and touch him. They allow us to communicate contemporaneously with Christ; they actually make Christ present to us. To celebrate a sacrament is not merely piously to commemorate a gesture of Christ; rather it is to exercise a power to make him return among us. "Come, Lord Jesus," said the primitive Christians in their liturgy.

St. Leo once said, "Ever since the Lord is not visible any more among us, all that was visible of him has passed into the sacraments." Christ's historical life was but the parable, the revelation of what was to happen forever: that God would always be among men, that men would ignore him and always mistreat him in the same manner. Christ was born but once because he was to be born over and over again. Every day the Word of God becomes flesh and dwells in our midst. Christ lived but once because he was to live forever. Christ suffered and was crucified once in order to suffer and to be persecuted forever. God is always the same, and men are always the same. He always comes among his own, and his own keep ignoring him. St. John wrote his Gospel purposely to celebrate Christ's presence in the sacraments. Already at that time, certain people regretted Christ's absence. John addressed his Gospel to them, warning them against the temptation to sentimentality which he labeled "scandalous." He once told them, "The time in which you are living now is the best;

21

Christ is better known now than he was then." All of St. John's Gospel was written to convey this message: it was of no avail to see Christ and to hear him. What was important was to believe; faith has always been urgent. "Blessed are they who have not seen, and yet have believed" (John 20, 29). It was to our advantage that Christ departed from us in his individual humanity in order that he might return as a vivifying spirit in all the sacraments of the Church, his body prolonged and communicable.

Time and time again, St. John affirmed that the apostles did not grasp what Christ was preaching; only later was his doctrine made clear to them. Even at the Last Supper, at the first Mass, Jesus said to Peter, "What I do thou knowest not now; but thou shalt know hereafter" (John 13, 7). At Mass, Peter finally understood the meaning of the Last Supper. The apostles lived a Christlike life only when they recognized him in the life, the worship, and the sacraments of the Church.

If John has written the most beautiful Gospel, it is precisely because he wrote it last. If John is so enlightening, it is not because he was the best witness from the beginning, but because he was privileged enough to be a more reliable witness on countless occasions. If he is such a good evangelist, it is simply because he had for a number of years celebrated the sacraments; he administered numerous baptisms and communions, and he contemplated the blood of the Eucharist and the water of baptism pouring forth from the open side of Christ on the cross.

The presence of Christ in the sacraments is infinitely more radiant, more efficacious, and more communicative than was his physical presence to his contemporaries. Do you want to assist at

22

his birth, his passion, and his resurrection? Simply witness a baptism, participate at Mass, or walk into a confessional.

It is there that Christ has decided to appear to you at all times. Christ will start anew in you that which he lived out for you only. Do not envy the people who lived in Our Lord's time. They ruined the whole plan; they did not want to recognize him, and they mistreated him. You complain that God is not visible enough. In those days, they also complained; they thought God did not manifest himself as he should. To complain that you did not live at that time is also the best proof that you are living at that time, that you are among those of whom Jesus said, "Forgive them, for they do not know what they are doing" (Luke 23, 34). Pay attention. You should know what you are doing; you are initiated, and you have been informed. This is what it means to be a Christian: to have received a revelation of what is happening all the time, to know that Christ becomes flesh and dwells in our midst until the consummation of the world.

The apostles lived this truth. They felt Christ dwelling in them as they spoke, when they celebrated the sacraments, and they continually marvelled at the fact that they were both doers and witnesses of such wonders. They testified to the accomplishment of the following promises: "I will not leave you orphans; I will come to you. . . . The Holy Spirit, whom the Father will send in my name, he will teach you all things, and bring to your mind whatever I have said to you" (John 14, 18. 26). What had formerly been a corporeal reality was now a spiritual experience. They never again felt nostalgic about the past when Jesus was physically present. They were happier now. St. Paul once proudly

23

said, "Even though we have known Christ according to the flesh, yet now we know him so no longer" (2 Corinthians, 5, 16). Ignatius of Antioch put it this way, "Heavenly things are so much more meaningful than material things. Even the Lord Jesus Christ manifests Himself so much more splendidly since He is at the right hand of the Father." These reflections are worthy of a Christian. "If you loved me, you would indeed rejoice that I am going . . ." (John, 14, 28).

Do we believe this? Do we know how fortunate we are? Why do we always look like victims or underdogs? We are God's spoiled children. Jesus is with us every day. There is nothing more impious than regret. Every time the apostles celebrated the sacraments, they delighted in his indubitable presence. They exercised the power that Christ himself had given them to make him present in their midst whenever they wished. Their wealth is ours. Our joy, our wonder, and our enthusiasm ought to be theirs.

3.

Death and Resurrection

Let us stop lamenting that we did not know Christ while he lived on earth. He is living here and now. Souvenirs hardly help us to accede to him, but baptism, penance, and holy Eucharist do. We should not attempt to unite ourselves to his earthly presence, but rather to his sacramental presence because he is more truly and more intensely present in the sacraments than he ever was in his physical existence. This sacramental presence is not only consoling but preferable. "It is expedient for you that I depart" (John 16, 7).

The sacraments are Christ's presence among us. He begins to live, to act, and to suffer anew, depending on our sluggishness, our dullness, slowness, and insouciance. The sacraments are Christ reincarnated until we awaken to what he does and what we do; until we are conscious of the way he treats us, and the manner we treat and mistreat him.

As the season of Lent opens, the passion starts all over again; today it mobilizes the same actors in the same roles as ever before.

To begin with, let us consider the millions and millions of indifferent and lazy people: those who are willing and those who wash their hands of guilt; those who do not budge unless they are concerned; those who refuse to express their opinion on moot questions and who let things be. If it were not for these people, if the wickedness of some were not endorsed by the cowardice of all, many evils would be non-existent. Before how many in-justices and dramatic scenes have we displayed criminal indif-ference?

And then, there are thousands of fugitives, people in difficult situations who, like St. Peter, ". . . do not know this man" (Matthew 26, 72). Yet, they have heard many sermons, they were moved to tears, they felt they were so good afterwards; they walked in funeral corteges, we saw them in processions. They were enthusiastic over miracles. They even walked far to witness one: they would have travelled to Lourdes, Rome, and Fatima. But now, when things go wrong, and all is sad; when there is blood and the cross; now that there are no more miracles, but it is our turn to be miracles of fidelity, faith, and love, they have nothing more to do with him. They do not know this man any more. They act as if they had never known him.

Thousands of tyrants exist; they are never lacking. They never change: the brute with his whip, the erudite with his biting criticism, the official with his regulations.

The infinitely patient and loving, dolorous Victim casts a tender, inquisitive, expectant, and reproachful look on us. More than ever there are victims: holy people who are suffering, inno-cent people who are persecuted; twelve million orphans, disabled war veterans, hundreds of displaced persons and incapacitated old people are offered in European public places, but there is no refuge for them. Thirty thousand Greek children are torn away from their parents and exiled by a fratricidal war, a real massacre of the innocents. Millions and millions of prisoners, it appears, are still living in concentration camps. There are millions of refugees and shelterless Koreans and Indochinese. Why go so

28

far? Here at home, around you, is there not anyone suffering and crying, someone cold and hungry? Is there no one who is sick; who grieves the death of a loved one; who suffers from solitude, sickness, or simply from his unfortunate character? These people are there; they wait, and they watch you. Who will be Veronica? Simon of Cyrene? Hurry. The roles are given out; it is impossible not to choose. Who will be John? Who will be Peter? Who will be Judas?

The Holy Spirit is the coach; he sees to it that the events of the life of Christ are relived in his members forever. The Gospels, that is, the good tidings, are the good news of the sacraments, namely, that Jesus is still living in our midst, that if we have not welcomed him today, that we can try again tomorrow and every day, for he is with us till the end of time.

Every sacrament is a participation in the destiny of Jesus which the Church sums up with painful sobriety: a death and a resurrection. He, who has said that there is no greater love than to give your life for those you love, invented the means of giving his life every day. Sacraments only serve this particular purpose: to communicate his life and permit us to diffuse it in turn, to give us life so that we may give it.

The sacraments replace and continue the miracles that God performed during his life. John calls all Christ's miracles "signs" because all had, besides their immediate efficacy, a more profound meaning.

When he narrates the cure of the man born blind, John well knew what blindness, a far more dangerous blindness, Christ would have to cure in so many people for centuries to come. When John narrates the cure of the paralytic, he is well aware of the many forms of paralysis of which we would all, and often, be relieved. No description is given which is not at the same time a prophecy, a prefiguration. When John describes the marriage at Cana, that banquet where water is changed into wine is already heavy with the news of another banquet where wine will be changed into blood.

This "sign" value of each narrative of St. John's Gospel has a permanent value. In the sacraments we seize the prolongation of these signs. If we know how to receive them properly, we attain a truth which is infinitely richer, infinitely more enlightening than those who saw only the historical fact. We are his contemporaries. Through the sacraments, he gave us the means, every time we desire it, to turn back the clock to the time he lived.

The sacraments are the efficacious signs of Christ's life. They produce in us what they commemorate in him. Whoever participates in a sacrament relives the life of Christ.

Baptism drowns us, destroys us, and plunges us into the Red Sea from which only the elect escape. It submerges us into the Jordan where the Son of God reveals himself in the midst of sinners, in this other baptism: "But I have a baptism to be baptized with; and how distressed I am until it is accomplished!" (Luke 12, 50). This is the baptism of blood on the cross. There is a way to die—imagine what luck that would be! There is a way to get rid of oneself, of this stupid and vicious individual who is insupportable to others and annoying to oneself. One can die. All that is necessary is to be baptized, to enter a confessional in order to die to our own wills, to our poor, sad, weak wills

30

that are our sins, and to resurrect to God's will that is love, faith, hope, sincerity, and righteousness.

Yes, we can resurrect in this very life. A baptized child is someone who is already dead, and who does not live his life, but that of Christ in him. Without doubt, our vitality is tenacious, and we must start over and over again before dying. We must keep on trying, time and time again, before we succeed in dying. But Christ's strength is still more tenacious. Nothing can efface this character of death and resurrection that baptism impressed on our souls and that each confession renews and each communion nourishes.

Mass is essentially a participation in the death and resurrection of Christ. The real "imitation of Christ," the true means to conform, to imitate his life, his passion, and his resurrection, is to participate in the Mass. Thus we shall imitate the obedience, the total devotedness of Christ to his Father. We shall become sons, brothers, nourishment in turn, bread that is offered and given, bread that is sacrificed and consecrated, bread that destroys itself to become a living Bread. We communicate to a body that has surrendered and to blood that has been shed. This body begins again to itself to us; this blood becomes, in the communicant, a spring, a fountain. He inspires us, in turn, to shed this blood for others as it was shed for us.

The Eucharist is so efficacious that it is capable of helping the entire world to participate in the death and the resurrection of Christ and thus help it cross from death to life in a final passover. To celebrate Mass is to hasten the end of the World. I do not believe that parishioners who assist at our Sunday Masses are very familiar with this idea. And yet, we say Mass that his kingdom may come. Even the next world becomes present at Mass. The Mass is a passover, a passage from one world to the next. The priest is a ferryman who offers to help all men who are willing to pass from a world of slavery to a free world, from a world of darkness to a world of light. When he started his first Mass, Jesus said, "The hour had come . . . to pass out of this world to the Father" (John 13, 1).

Perhaps the world will not end in a cataclysm, an annihilation, a catastrophe. Possibly, the world will end in a Eucharistic feast. When holy Eucharist will be celebrated by the whole world, then this world will pass, and the Lord will manifest himself in all his glory. When the primitive Christians had received communion, they knelt and said, "May the world pass now, and may your kingdom come." They had passed over. They were so delighted with the world of the Father that they wished never to turn back. They were naturalized to "divine things," and they preferred them to all else forever.

4.

Brotherhood

The Church makes the sacraments, but the sacraments make the Church. They create the Christian community. The role of the sacraments is not merely to unite us to God, but also to unite us indivisibly to one another. As they help us share God's life, they instruct us to share men's lives, and they fill us with God's love to teach us to love one another.

Each sacrament is communal. In spite of appearances, "a private communion" or "a private Mass" does not exist. Confession is not a whispering-in-the-dark, but a rehabilitation in the Church. Baptism, far from being a confidential ceremony of purely family interest, is or ought to be a parochial and fraternal feast.

Christians today are conscious of their solidarity. They are no longer individualists. The drama of our century consists precisely in this: before the world that tries, as hard as it can, to establish a fraternity without a Father, the Christian believes in the Fatherhood of God without the brotherhood of man. Yet, Christian religion is essentially fraternal. The son, separated from his brothers, is not a son any more, and God ignores him. Separate yourself from the community of your brothers, and you immediately cut yourself from the condition of son of God. You are not any closer to God than you are to your neighbor.

Christian Pharisaism consists in wanting to unite to God whom we do not see, while refusing to unite to our brother whom we see. Too often, our good relations with God console us for our poor relations with our brothers. When a woman turns to piety, we wonder whether or not she is getting along with her husband. If it is the husband who is pious, you will find people who think that he must not get along with anyone.

Christ reversed all these values. He once said that you have the same relations with God as with your neighbor. You are not any closer to God than you are to your neighbor. The only proof that you love God is that you also love your neighbor.

Christ wanted to make us capable of loving one another. There is something greater and more difficult than loving God, or rather, the love of God lends itself to countless illusions. We do not see God, we invent him; we imagine him; we focus on him, and we get closer to him or farther away from him at will. We create him according to our fancy, at our convenience, if not according to our resemblance. He tolerates the situation. He is silent, but others are not so tolerant. It is impossible to see them as we fancy. They are not silent. If husband and wife are silent, they pull a long face that is more eloquent than words. Also, there is in Christianity a kind of priority of the love of neighbor over the love of God: "If thou art offering thy gift at the altar, and there rememberest that thy brother has anything against thee, leave thy gift before the altar and go first to be reconciled to thy brother, and then come and offer thy gift" (Matthew 5, 23–24).

That is why sacraments indivisibly unite us to God and neighbor. When you were baptized, you became a member of Christ's body. You wanted to unite to God, and we united you to your brothers. You took part in Christ's death, and that was the death of your self-love. You took part in the resurrection of Christ, and you discovered such a new self that you were able to love others. For you, to adhere to God signifies: to start adhering to others. And God's absence, of which you complained so much in your life, is perhaps nothing else than the absence of your brothers.

However, through baptism, we are more brothers and sisters than if we had been born of the same mother. With our deep-seated individuality, we magnify our miserable differences: I am rich, he is poor; I am intelligent, he is stupid; I belong to such and such a family, he belongs to another. We forget our similarity: he belongs to Christ, and so do I. He is Christ's very own, and so am I.

Which one of us would accept to become his neighbor: next-door neighbor, neighbor at table, in church or at work? And yet, if that neighbor is incorporated in Christ, why should we not become anybody, if he is Christ's very own? We become hard-to-please, refined, and fastidious. But when communion is distributed to all these people with whom we do not want to associate, this is precisely what is happening to Christ. He accepts to become anybody. He gives himself to anyone who accepts him in his life, who wants to be with him forever. God does not play hard-to-please. God makes us his brothers and sisters.

When you receive holy communion, you do not communicate to God alone, but also to all those who are united to him, who happen to belong, like you, to his body. You will not save yourself by accepting to swallow God. You must also swallow all the others. It is useless to say: So-and-so, I shall not swallow him; I cannot bear him. How can you pretend to communicate to Christ's body if you reject his members?

Certainly, we are far from realizing that. Even our communions have become individualistic: each one for himself and God for all. Each one piously elaborates his solitary meditation, with fists closed over his eyes to better isolate himself. He seems to say, "Let no one speak to me. Let no one touch me. Leave me alone. I am communicating." We isolate ourselves, we keep aloof from others, we excommunicate ourselves in the very act by which we pretend to communicate.

And yet, by instituting holy Eucharist, the Lord wanted us to unite among ourselves as much as to unite to him. "That all may be one, even as thou, Father, in me and I in thee" (John 17, 21). We receive his love to live it. We are not so sure of having known God's love unless we, in turn, love one another. The only indication that we have validly assisted at Mass is that we love one another more after Mass than we did before.

As for confession, try to figure this out: to be sure that we are very much alone, we shut up in a closet; yet, confession is in itself a communal act. "Forgive us our sins, for we also forgive everyone who is indebted to us" (Luke 11, 4). There is no pardon from the Father if you do not forgive your brothers. There is only one thing that God can not forgive: our refusal to forgive. For you have not learned forgiveness if you are unable to forgive. You have not learned love if you do not know how to love. You are reconciled to the whole Church at the same time that you are reconciled to God. The entire Church forgives you. You are reinstated in the love of the Father at the same time that you join in communion with your brothers. You become as close to others as you have become close to God.

5.

Baptism

As we enter a church, we sometimes see in one of the lateral chapels a group of people around a baby who is to be baptized. Immediately, we very discreetly turn from the scene, not to disturb the privacy of this family ceremony.

But this is absurd and regrettable. We have a greater right to belong to this child's family than any other person around him. We who are baptized are more brothers and sisters than if we were born of the same mother and father. We not only belong to the same family but also to the same body. What is going on in this chapel concerns us; this baby is going to be bound, aggregated, and incorporated to us, to this body of which we are a part. He pledges to live a life of love and union with us. We ought to be there; that Sunday afternoon, all of us should be there at the baptism to celebrate the incarnation of Christ in this child of our parish, with as much joy and solemnity as we celebrated Christ's presence in the Eucharistic feast that morning at Mass. Is not Christ really present in this baptized child? Is not this presence more faithful, more durable, and more "expressive" than his presence in bread?

We should not let him incorporate himself to the Church *solo*. We constitute the body of Christ. Whom will this child be related to if we are not there? The effect of baptism is to carry the child over from the state of sin, where people do not love one another, to the world of Christ, to Christian brotherhood, where people love one another. Families would do well to profit by a baptism to solemnly reconcile with each other. To what kind of Church, to what kind of community will they incorporate this baby?

I sometimes wonder if many of my pupils have ever met the Church, or if they ever discovered a milieu where generous and convinced adults love one another. What is the point in baptizing them if we do not incorporate them?

Certainly they will become children of God, but where will they meet his family? Surely they will receive grace, but this grace consists in loving others, and where will they learn how to put it in practice? So many of our Christians belong to their social class more than to their Christian brotherhood. Whether they are laborers or middle-class people, they are framed, ingrained in their social, racial, and oftentimes even in their religious prejudices which isolate and embitter them, often separating them from others forever. The exorcism ceremony of baptism is certainly not superfluous to conjure these divisions and to allow us to overcome them some day.

Christ's desire is not to unite us to him alone but to unite us with one another: "That all may be one" (John 17, 21). He is never present in the life of someone that seeks him while he is excluding others. But he intensely lives where there are two or three united in his name. All who have lived in the true Church in a sincere brotherhood have experienced the faith and joy resulting thereof. Our faith and especially that of our children depend first of all on a joyous, friendly, and fervent Christian community of which we are a member. The absence of God, of which so many people complain, is perhaps the absence of our brothers. Christ's religion is made to be lived only in the Church.

However, it does not shut us in. The true dimension of our Christian vocation is not the Church but the universe. The Church is a grouping of people with different vocations; the Church is a convocation for the salvation of the entire world.

We are not baptized to assure our individual salvation in a headlong flight. Nor are we baptized to seek refuge in the Church, sheltered from the dangers of this wicked world. Salt is made to pour out of the salt shaker, and yeast to go into dough. A Catholic milieu is a contradiction in terms. The Christian community has no other limit but humanity. The true Christian milieu is the world, this world which God loves so much that each morning he sends his sons and daughters to save it. All the power of faith, unity, and love of the Church must be put at the service of those who are still out of the Church.

Too many Christians ignore their apostolic vocation. Baptism does not guarantee us a reserved seat in heaven; it enlists us for the evangelization of the world and makes us workers and collaborators of God. He who is intent on saving his own soul will lose it. The servant who has received a talent and returns it to his master, very clean and wrapped in a cloth, hears his master tell him, "Where are the others?" and he is condemned.

Because it conforms us to Christ, baptism must make of us people who save, much more than people who are saved. At the Last Judgment, the following question will resound as it did at the beginning: "Where is your brother Abel? . . . what have you done?" (Genesis 4, 9. 10). St. Augustine aptly comments, "It is strange that when I step on your foot, your tongue shouts. Well, take care, at the day of reckoning, your Head will reproach you what you have done to his members."

The Church does not pretend to organize religious ceremonies that lull the devout and make people think that all goes well. She has a more important task to perform: she is responsible for the salvation of the world. She feeds her children, forms them and instructs them, not for the purpose of pampering them in a peaceful nursery, but to send them into the world as beneficent missiles. Too many Christians believe that we must live to eat; by this I mean that, for them, to frequent the sacraments is at the same time the proof and the crowning of their Christian vitality. But we only eat to live; we must feed on God in order to give him to others. God must live in us so that others will recognize him through us.

Such is your Christian vocation. It would be a wearisome burden if we ignored that when God calls, he gives what is necessary to answer. At baptism we alone did not vow ourselves to his service; it is he who pledged to help us. We are unfaithful, he is faithful; we are inconstant, but he perseveres. We renew our baptismal promises at the Easter vigil, but God permits us to relive them at each communion. Time and time again, he reminds us of what he has asked us, so we end up answering his call. Our Christian fidelity springs from our baptismal vocation.

6.

Holy Eucharist

I.

The real name for holy Mass is Eucharist, that is, thanksgiving and gratitude. We do not go to Mass to receive favors; we go to give thanks. There is a great misunderstanding that needs clarification. The faithful are bored at Mass because they want it to be profitable to them, to serve their purpose, and to obtain favors for them. But the Mass was instituted to praise God and to give thanks to him. How many people have never entered into that fundamental movement of restitution, joy, and thanksgiving that should elevate our entire life and that fully expresses itself at Mass!

The essential of religion is to believe in God's love for us and to rejoice at the thought of what he did for us. First of all, religion does not consist in what we do for God, in the sad, poor, and trivial things that we sacrifice or accomplish for him. Religion consists in the wonders of fidelity, generosity, and mercy that God does for us. Religion is ecstasy, wonder, and joy. And so, it becomes naturally a Eucharist, that is, a thanksgiving. Holy Eucharist is the movement by which we are drawn to God by that very power with which he gives himself to us.

For if God had only permitted us to receive, he would not have given us any part of himself. As for him, his function is not to receive but to be gift and love. Also, if God gives himself entirely to us, if he totally trusts us, if he reveals the nature of his being and the taste of his joy, it is understood that he must give us the power to give.

Man has a more profound need than that of receiving. He, in turn, can get enthusiastic, and at once he can give all he has ever received. That is the Eucharist.

Christ essentially constitutes the Eucharist. When he tells his Father, "All things that are mine are thine, and thine are mine" (John 17, 10), he is not passing a reflection, nor inventing a means of showing his gratitude. He expresses an identity. For the particular attributes of the Father are to love and to give. So what the Son has received is the power to give. His own devotedness to the Father is also a revelation of the manner in which the Father loves him. Where did he learn so much love? From his Father: "I do what I have seen with the Father" (see John 8, 38). He continually gives thanks for what he has received, for what he has learned from him.

From time immemorial, the Word of God is a perfect, total, and joyous Eucharist. George MacDonald says, "When he was crucified, he did that in the wild weather of his outlying provinces which he had done at home in glory and gladness." At Calvary, Christ gave himself; he commended his spirit into the hands of the Father: "Father, into thy hands I commend my spirit (Luke 23, 46). For an instant, in the solemn march of the centuries, heaven opened, and we assisted at God's eternal beatitude. We saw how God loves, and to what extent he knows how to love. We called this Calvary, passion, suffering, and death; but it was really only the Eucharist.

48

At Mass, we Christians are drawn into the Son's Eucharist; we are initiated to God's divine ways, to the beautiful courtesies of God's dwelling. As we see Jesus offer thanksgiving, we also start to realize that if God loved us so, suffered so, and worked for us, we ought to be won over by his generosity and confide ourselves to him as he confided himself to us.

We solemnly remit him that which he gave us: his most precious gift, his Son, and it is through him, with him, and in him that we render him all honor and glory. That is why we communicate to Christ: so that we may be incorporated to his obedience, to participate in his death to self and to his resurrection in God in order to be nothing else but thanksgiving.

To believe that it is worthy and just, equitable, and salutary to give thanks always and everywhere is the greatest act of faith. The Church repeats this at requiem Masses and at nuptial Masses.

This is the most joyous act in the world. It reinstates us to our true nature. It reshapes us into this willing filial being we become each time we accept to be a new person, each time we accept, after having surrendered all, to receive everything anew. It restores us to God and to ourselves, to the individual God wants us to be.

The Mass is not a homage to the real presence of Christ in our midst. It is a participation, an entrance into his death and resurrection. We must die to self in order to feel nothing but gratitude and wonder. We must not be self-centered, but live only of the life of God in order to find nothing else living in us but joy for others, the pride of the Magnificat: God has done great things because of the poverty of his servants.

49

II.

The altar, regardless of its decoration, size, or shape, is, first of all, a table. On this table, in preparation for the meal, are put the tablecloth, the bread, the wine, some water, a cup, a golden plate, and some flowers. Both the priest and the faithful are invited to eat flesh that is food indeed, and to drink blood that is drink indeed.

What do you do at a meal?

No, you have not guessed correctly. You do not begin by eating. You do not hurry to sample all the dishes, you do not sit down at the table immediately. You begin with conversation, and that is precisely what happens at Mass.

What does one speak about? Well, very often people begin by excusing themselves if they have come late, or if one has just lately said or done something not so polite, perhaps towards one's hosts. "I confess to Almighty God . . ."

Then we sometimes profit by the occasion to ask some little service: Can you lend me such-and-such? Will you send me this information? Could you go to see So-and-so? The Kyrie litany is chanted for the many needs of the Church.

At times we exchange news. Look: I have just received a letter from a friend of ours. Thus we read from an epistle of the blessed Paul, James, Peter, or John.

Sometimes the most venerable person in the assembly speaks a few words and every one listens with respect. He reads from the Gospel according to St. John, or of one of the evangelists. And when he has finished, all voice their approval and admiration. Credo. I believe. That is also my opinion. I agree wholeheartedly.

Then, at a repast, one offers. Guests often show their pleasure and gratitude and esteem for their host by bringing him a gift— chocolates, a basket of fruit, a bottle of good wine, something that shows that they appreciate the invitation and that they desire to share in the feast. And the host places upon the table the best that he has in order to show honor to his guests.

But alas! at Mass hardly anybody shows this little attention. You should be preoccupied a day or two before with the thought of what you can bring, or send, which would show God your joy in coming, your gratitude for being invited, and your desire to participate in the joy of this feast.

Happily, there are some brave souls with kindly hearts who sweep the church, who offer flowers, who make up bouquets. God is not totally neglected. There are still a few here and there who treat him as a person with a heart that is capable of suffering or of rejoicing, who regard him as a Father.

And at the end, naturally, one eats, one participates, one communicates. The meal at table is the time for the whole family to come together. When you wish to establish or renew relations with some person or friend, or bring a group of friends closer together, or when you celebrate a marriage, or want to manifest your good will, you invite these people to your table and eat with them.

And so with the Mass. Once a week the Father of the family, our Father in heaven, assembles his children. He reunites his poor, anxious children, so taken up by their cares and weaknesses, and he reminds them that they have a Father. Even though they may be grown up or well on in years, they still have a Father in heaven. Even though they may be feeble and sinful, they are still the sons of God. To him they are still children. Though they have spent the past week in working, in spending themselves, he still awaits them each Sunday to comfort them, to renew their strength, and to place in their hearts all the love that they are going to need for others. For we are so poor in love that, in order to love our wives, or husbands, our parents, our children, our friends as they expect us to love them, we need nothing less than God himself, God's love in our hearts, so that we may be capable of giving all the love that is required of us.

The Father makes us sit at his table. He makes himself known to us in the breaking of the bread, in the same way that a father or a mother so often wins the recognition and the love of their children in the gay family meals, and he makes them recognize themselves as his own children.

God calls man to lift up his head. He reminds him that he is not made for this earth and for this heavy toil, that he is made to love, to think, to know, to believe, to hope, to create, to admire; that he is the beloved child of God, and that his destiny is to be eternally happy in the company of his Father and of his brethren, all united in the one same love.

What would you think of a child who was reluctant to go to, who dislikes to be in his Father's house, who limits his presence to the shortest possible length of time, and, worst of all, if he consents to go, refuses to eat at his table? There are many children of God who are still willing to go to their Father's house but who refuse to eat at his table. They are not hungry, this bread says nothing to them, they have no confidence in this nourishment, they have eaten, as a precaution, before they came, they say that they cannot swallow a mouthful, and there they are, throughout the meal, sitting mournfully in front of an empty plate. How the mistress of the house must feel about guests like that! They are enough to take the appetite away from all the other guests. What a miserable meal it would be if a goodly number of the guests refused to associate or to communicate in the gaiety and friendliness of the others. Who among you would bother to invite people so wanting in good manners, or celebrate a feast under like conditions? And the Father invites us to his table every Sunday.

The Mass was, in the beginning, a repast, a true meal, a friendly and fraternal gathering at which Christ spoke at length with his disciples. At the close of a friendly meal, the guests are expansive and become confidential and reserve is abandoned. It was at this Last Supper that Jesus said to his apostles, "Now I will no longer call you servants but friends, for all that I have heard from my Father I have made known to you."

At this repast, Jesus gave the best that he had, his own flesh to nourish us, his own blood for a transfusion of blood, his own life for a transfusion of life.

And all of them communicated and they communicated together. What joy and what fervor must have been theirs after their first communion! They felt that they were so transported with love and fraternal joy, so lifted above themselves and their egoism, so cured of their isolation, that they knew for certain that God alone could do this, that only God could love them thus. For the first time they overflowed with enthusiasm and confidence and they said to Jesus, "Now we see that you know all things and we believe that you came forth from God."

When shall we, too, as we leave after our Sunday Mass, find ourselves so happy, so renewed, so fraternal, so generous, that we know beyond all doubt that God alone could change us like this, that God was present among us, that we have seen the Father and that that is sufficient for us?

OUR PARTICIPATION IN THE MASS

The Mass is a feast at which the Father of the family tries to reassemble his children in order to renew the family spirit. It is the joy of the Father to be surrounded by his sons and daughters. Of course, it is he who provides the meal, but it is also he who rejoices the most at seeing them about him, all happy and eating with good appetite the food which he has provided for them.

What kind of a meal would it be if the children came late; if one after the other so calculated the time as not to arrive even one minute in advance; if they refused to take part in the conversation; and would not answer when someone asked them a question or merely spoke to them; if they brought no gift to show their pleasure, not even a little flower or a thank you; and if they refused to eat, declaring that they were not hungry, that they had no appetite, but sat there, mute, before their empty plates?

One would have to be God to put up with that. We would very soon have led them to the door and have invited others the next time.

Only a Father, the Father, would suffer that with patience and prefer to see them again, even like that, rather than not see them at all.

But, as to ourselves, what good would it do us to be present at a meal without taking part in it? Would you be content to contemplate the meal of others and then declare that you were well fed and strengthened? To assist passively at a Mass likewise does us no good. If the Mass were active and sanctifying all by itself, without any participation on our part, then the sacristans and the ushers would be the greatest saints in the whole Church. They have assisted at the greatest number of Masses, they have broken all records for assistance at Mass.

The one indispensable condition for making our Masses fruitful is that we act, that we respond, that we put ourselves into it, that we take part in the Mass.

At each Mass the early Christians made four processions. The first took place at the entrance. (They waited outside, gathered together, formed the body of Christ before they entered.) The second procession was at the offertory, and the third at the communion. (Everyone received communion. They would not have dreamed of coming to Mass without going to communion!) The last procession took place when they were leaving.

Their Masses were not celebrated in silence. They made the responses, and with a loud voice too. The Fathers of the Church say that, in the Roman basilicas, at the time of the elevation, the "Amen" of the congregation was like the roar of thunder.

They participated generously in the sacrifice. At the offertory, at the time when we sit down, they got up and went procession-ally to the altar, to bring their offering, while we go searching in our purse or pocket for the smallest coin that we have. They brought to God something that they judged worthy of being given to God and which made them partakers in the sacrifice. The altar was covered with offerings—heaps of bread, fruit, or gifts of other kind that could be distributed to the poor.

The offering became a representation of each; there, on the altar, each one was present through the intermediary of his gift; each one prayed and believed that the same transformation would be accomplished in himself as that which was about to take place in his gift.

They would have been ashamed to communicate in the sacri-fice offered by another. They would have felt like parasites, spongers, profiting by the sacrifice of another rather than provid-ing their own. For many among us is not the Mass a "painless sacrifice" where one expects to benefit by the sacrifice of Christ, dispensed thereby from making one of his own?

The boredom, the sterility of our Masses comes from our avarice. We are not a part of it. Our motive for coming to Mass should not be principally to ask for grace, but to give thanks, to give oneself, to please God and one's brethren and to find pleasure in giving them pleasure.

He who gives nothing to anyone is in condition to receive nothing from anyone.

The Hindu poet, Rabindranath Tagore, tells this parable:

I was going begging from door to door along the street of the village when your gilded chariot appeared in the distance. It was like to a dream, a splendid thing, and I admired him who was the king of kings. My hopes rose high and I thought: This is the end of my misery. I was already sure that I would receive large alms, offered spontaneously, and that coins would be scattered about me in the dust.

Your chariot stopped there where I was standing.

Your glance fell upon me and you alighted and smiled at me. I felt that the chance of a lifetime had come to me.

Then, suddenly, you held out your hand to me and said to me: What have you to give me?

Ah, what royal game was this? To come begging from a beggar?

I was bewildered and then perplexed, and finally, from my sack, I took a tiny grain of wheat and I gave it to you.

You went on your way, but what was my surprise when, at the end of the day, I emptied my sack out on the ground, I found a grain of gold amid the grains of wheat. Then did I weep and I thought: Why did I not have the courage to give you all that I had!

And so with us. Only that which we have offered will be preserved. Is it not true that, so far, our Masses have brought us only what they have cost us, and that is mighty little?

We have become so civilized that we have invented an economical sacrifice, one in which nothing is offered. We pompously declare to God that we offer ourselves entirely to him. To offer our possessions, that is too little for us, and, besides, it is vulgar. We offer ourselves! It sounds very beautiful to say that, but it

58

would be useful to verify from time to time the sincerity of this consecration by taking a dollar or two from our purse to see how detached we really are.

C. S. Lewis has said, "Each morning I offer to God all my day. But before I have finished shaving that day has become all mine again, to such an extent that the few moments of it that I will consecrate to God seem to me to be taken from my personal fortune and not without pain, and God seems to me to usurp whatever he takes from me."

Our ancestors, whom we designate as savages, knew more about sacrifice than we do, we who in our civilization feel only contempt for their bloody sacrifices.

And yet, when they felt themselves cut off from God, unhappy and alone, they knew how to reëstablish contact. They did not offer, as we do, sham sacrifices, handsome imitations. They took their fastest horse, the cow that gave most milk, the truest arrow, their warmest cloak, and they immolated it, consumed it, offered it to God. And looking up to God with ardor they said to him, "I have more confidence in you than in that for my nourishment; I have more confidence in you than in that for my protection; I have more confidence in you than in all my goods, or in myself, for the protection of my life!"

As for us, our goods and possessions permit us to do without God. To have everything that we need is a terrible thing, for it proves that we have no need of God.

Our money protects us from God. If I give, if I make an offering, that means that I am removing a piece of my armor. I am rendering myself vulnerable to Providence!

How do you stand with God? Do you expect something from him? Do you feel a need for him?

As long as you have not placed in God's keeping something dear to you, as long as you have not placed on God's altar some person or some thing that belongs to you, you do not cling to God, for there where your true treasure is, there also is your heart!

Who is there among us who is so devoted to the Mass, so represented, so present on the altar, that he can hope that the same transformation will be accomplished in him as in his gift?

If nothing of yours is given to God, if there is nothing to represent you on the altar, there will be no change in you. You need not hide near the door in order to get out quickly in case anything should happen. There is no danger whatever. You will leave again just as you came. Your purse will be the same and so will be your heart!

The French Canadians whose losses were great during World War II had a deep understanding of this. Instead of establishing cemeteries for their dead, they requested that the battlefield where so many of their sons, their fathers, their husbands and brothers were killed, should be sown with wheat, and from the wheat that was harvested there, they made hosts. The widows, the orphans, the parents who mourned for these men knew, when they offered their hosts at Mass, what they had given to God. They knew where their treasure was and who it was who watched over it. And when they received communion they found again, united in Christ, all those whom they had lost but whom they would find again because they had been offered. And as they returned, their hearts filled with God and their loved ones, eternal life was begun for them, where there would never again be separation, sorrow, and tears.

Everyone finds again in the Mass what he has offered, what he loves, what he has loved sufficiently to offer, and, in doing so, to render it eternal.

7.

Penance

There is no sacrament without joy. The sacrament of penance is, in a way, the most joyous of all since it restores a soul to God. So it is considered in heaven where a sinner who has been granted forgiveness causes more joy than ninety-nine just who have no need of pardon. But it rarely produces this effect on earth; rather, it has stopped producing it. In Christ's lifetime, each of his pardons would end with a banquet. Zacchaeus, Matthew, and the prodigal son celebrated their reconciliation at table with their Confessor. These customs are not ours any longer, and you will rarely see your father or your husband return home to celebrate, with his family, the pardon that gave him joy. Christ gaily invited himself at the table of sinners before inviting them, in turn, to the holy communion table.

We have carefully partitioned these two tables, to the point of making of the first a kind of closet where we steal away discreetly, the less often, the better. The origin of this disaffection is perhaps the same as that of boredom at Mass: ignorance of God's wonders. We always believe that religion is what we do for God: our difficult and worrisome examination of conscience, the entrance into the confessional box where we go to hide . . . in public, the avowal of our sins and the penance to be recited. All this is burdensome, disagreeable, and irritating.

Quite the contrary! Penance is God's pardon; it is the great things that God does for us: the manifestation of his kindness and of his love that is seen nowhere better than in this supreme gift which is pardon. "If we were not sinners, more in need of pardon than of bread, we would ignore the depth of God's heart." Before they have been sick, children do not know the extent of their mother's devotedness. God is grace, but when shall we better know it than when he pardons? God alone can forgive sins: God alone can make each of our faults a happy fault because we shall always remember the paternal tenderness that was revealed on this occasion.

We have reduced the sacrament to the measure of our acts. We must enlarge it to the measure of God's act. If you had met Christ with your regular list of faults, you would have immediately understood that you could not tell him anything that you generally confess, because it was too insignificant and useless. You would have known instantly that he was living, that he knew you, that he loved you personally, that you never believed him and that this was your real fault.

Under Our Lord's gaze, brilliant with affection and indulgence, so understanding and encouraging, we would have known our deficiencies. We would have recognized our greatest fault which we should, before all else, accuse and which explains all the rest: not to have known who he was and not to have really believed in his existence and his love.

We would immediately have understood what we lacked up to this moment, that which we had suffered from without being able to pinpoint it. Certainly, our life was empty without him, and we had to fill this void with something, even if it had to be sins for which we did not care too much, of which we were not too proud, but which were indispensable in this sad life that

66

we are living, sins to which we had a right, after all, with all the worries that overwhelm us. What would we have had in our life if we had not had our sins?

But if Jesus loved us, if this love filled and transfigured our life; if we could believe that we are followed, supported, and filled with such a love, then we would realize that we have all we need. We do not have to sin any more; it is useless. We do not feel like sinning; we are too happy thus.

However, that is what confession is: an encounter with Christ, a contact with Christ, an experience of his extraordinary power of resurrection and life: "Lazarus, come forth!" (John 11, 43). "Young man, I say to thee, arise" (Luke 7, 14). "Go in peace. Thy sins are forgiven" (Luke 7, 48).

Penance is a discovery of the kindness and love of the Father. God tells us but one thing in his sacramental absolution: that he loves us, that he forgives us, that our repentance and his grace make us his children once more. The priest is not delegated for any other message than to tell us that God loves us much more than we rejoice to be absolved. And it is this love, the revelation of this kindness, which slowly awakens love in our heart. He to whom we do not forgive does not love; he to whom we forgive little loves little; he to whom we forgive much inevitably sees the day when he will have learned to love much.

When the prodigal son decided to return to his father and ask for his forgiveness, his heart was dead to affection. He believed that he was no longer loved. He did not believe he was his son; he returned to eat at the servants' table, in a remoteness which he accepted. Long before the boy had thought of returning, the father had been waiting for him. The father embraced his son;

he did not give him any time to finish his confession, but called his servants to dress him in fine clothes, and to celebrate his homecoming. In his father's arms, he surprisingly felt himself becoming a son once again. His father's love restored him to this condition, and when he saw how his father loved him, he surprisingly learned over again to love as a son loves his father.

We also are lost. We seem to ignore that we have a Father. We shall find ourselves once again in the position of sons only in the arms of the Father. For when God tells us, as he forgives us, that he loves us, he does more than just tell us. He communicates with us; he creates his love in us, and we begin to know how he loves us by experimenting the love with which we begin to love him. For we are so poor, so sterile, and so weak, that we can love only with the love that he will have awakened in our hearts by revealing and communicating his love to us.

8.

Authority

We easily admit that the Church has sacraments. That she gives life, restores it, and fortifies it does not rouse anyone's indignation. That the Church has dogmas makes the situation less tolerable. To begin with, there are certitudes that challenge the intelligence and that the intelligence cannot challenge, truths which, I admit, transcend what I have understood of them because I trust the one who has transmitted them to me; all this irritates me. But when I reflect, are these truths any different from what I already accept in other fields where I believe in experiments that I did not repeat, or facts that I have not verified?

But if the Church gives me orders, if she has a government, if she exercises authority, many people seem to think this is unacceptable, too worldly; it assimilates the Church to political power and compromises her.

Far from it; all this really assimilates the Church to Christ. The Church governs simply because she prolongs Christ, and Christ directs her. Among the faithful the Church exercises that same power which Christ exercised among his apostles. The Church would cease to be Christ if she did not imitate him. The foundation of obedience to the Church is our faith in the fact that there is no other means to adhere to God and to obey God and to remain united to those to whom he said, "He who hears you, hears me" (Luke 10, 16). "Whatever thou shalt bind on earth shall be bound in heaven" (Matthew 16, 19).

The Lord submitted us to men only to subject us more securely to God. To want to obey an invisible God in his heaven does not suffice. What guarantee have I that his will, as I conceive it, will not be the product of my interests, my imagination, or my fancy? How can I be certain that, as I pretend to obey God, I am not obeying myself? Christ gave us this means, this guarantee: he told us to obey God as he manifested himself on earth, to obey the incarnate God of history and the true living God, who is with us every day until the consummation of the world.

Thus, we submit ourselves neither to our caprices nor to the whims of our leaders. Our obedience is always directed, through them, to him who designated these leaders for us, and who made our union with them a sign of our union with him. "That all may be one . . . that the world may believe that thou hast sent me" (John 17, 21).

As they obey the Church, the faithful continue Christ's obedience to his Father. When the hierarchy commands, it continues the mission that the Father entrusted to his Son: "As the Father has sent me, I also send you" (John 20, 21).

But this power which the Church holds from Christ must be exercised as he exercised it: as the good shepherd who does not govern with an iron rod, who came, not to be served, but to serve. Her leader is meek and humble of heart. He does not seek his glory. The Church must sacrifice herself prodigiously to yield the terrible power of ruling without yielding to corruption through hardness, pride, and interest.

The jurisdiction of the Church exacts more sanctity than any other of her powers. As for the sacraments, the task is easy: luckily, their efficacy does not depend on the moral value of the minister. I receive baptism or holy Eucharist just as validly from the hands of an unworthy priest as from the hands of a saint because both of them are, as far as sacraments are concerned, only Christ's instruments.

The power of authority is already less secure; the extent of its infallibility is restricted. There is but a small number of dogmas, and the rest of the teaching of the Church is a function of the value of the men who compose her. But the government itself is by no means infallible. Although it benefits by the Holy Spirit, it is still subject to error, and it has but one ultimate and indiscernible guarantee: whatever errors the Church commits, she will never perish. Christ subjects us to fallible men. We must not disregard our duty of obedience to them nor their fallibility.

The role of the faithful is to help authority by an intelligent, active, and vigilant obedience. A passive obedience is fundamentally a passive resistance. Obedience does not dispense anyone from action or from reflection. Too many faithful act in the Church as shareholders in anonymous societies: they share dividends, but this is the only manifestation of their interest in the affairs of the societies. Such an abdication is blameworthy. The greatest disservice to authority consists in a servility that invites it to authoritarianism. The clericalism of which we reproach priests is often nothing more than the consequence of the laymen's passivity. We are all responsible in the Church. The Church forms us, and we form the Church. We must think, search, cooperate actively with and expose our views to authority, keep it informed, and even present our objections. Obedience to the Church is a duty of conscience, and not an invitation to unconsciousness.

Precisely because the divine guarantee is less, our vigilance must

73

be greater, and responsibilities must be shared on a greater scale. We cannot content ourselves with a passive submission by abandoning all the burden of action to the hierarchy. Church jurisdiction exacts a final obedience, but not a total confidence. Each of the faithful must feel that he is the Church and implement in his life the general principles inculcated by the Church.

We should never allow ourselves to be separated from the Church: unity is a good, superior to all others because it is the sign of love. But let us not hide from each other her imperfections and faults: this would be the surest means of failing in our duty to remedy the situation.

If the Church seems alien to the modern man, if she often seems to be ill-adapted and slow-moving, it is because Christ's presence has not been assured to our contemporaries. Millions of nominal Christians live as people always lived, like everybody else, instead of being conscious of their responsibility to incarnate Christ in today's world.

9.

The Word

Some months ago the Apostleship of Prayer recommended Family Bible Reading as its monthly intention. I hope that you pray for the intentions of the Apostleship of Prayer; but I presume that that month it was not with much enthusiasm.

There are, of course, families who read the Scriptures. I know of one in which, every week, the parents and two eldest children select a page of the Gospels, read a commentary on the full textual meaning of that passage, and then, each day, meditate on that passage for ten minutes. They "listen" to it. The following Sunday they come together and say quite simply what that text has suggested to them.

Does that seem extraordinary?

St. Paul, in his epistle to the Colossians, expresses the wish that "the word of Christ may live in you" so that you may live in it. "Man does not live by bread alone but by every word that comes from the mouth of God" (Matthew 4, 4).

Is it not much more extraordinary that the word of God, the message which God sends us, his "Good News," is something that we find dull and uninteresting?

God has written to us, and we put his letter into our pocket and leave it there. God has left us his "testament," and we are so persuaded that there is nothing in it that we do not even read it.

There is one book that Christians never read. There is one

book which, if you are not careful, you will die without having read. Of all the books in my library, there is one which I am perfectly certain will never be borrowed. I have no fear whatever that I shall lose it. My visitors are interested in all my books except that one. No one has any desire to read it, no curiosity towards it; each one is sure that there is nothing in it for him. That book, of course, is the Gospel.

All this indifference is going to cause us some embarrassment when we get to heaven. When we meet our Lord, and are welcomed by him with so much affection, so much joy, so much attention, and we see his face glowing so with goodness and tenderness, and see him so intimate with each one of us, we shall be overcome by our amazement. We shall cry out regretfully, "Lord, if I had but known! If I had only known you! If only someone had told me that you were like this! My whole life would have been so different! Never would I have given in to sadness and discouragement. I would have told the whole world about you and won everyone over to you. Why is it that no one ever told me of this?"

And Christ will reply, "How does it happen that you did not know? I know well that the sermons of my priests are not always remarkable, but I took care to leave a very faithful portrait of myself, a most exact description. Haven't you read the Gospel?"

He will be insistent. "Were you so occupied that you did not have time to read? What did you do with your free time? What other books have you read? What did you find more urgent, or more important?"

Do you see yourself giving an explanation? Do you see yourself naming the titles of the books that you have read?

We call ourselves Christians because we have found no life more beautiful, no person more holy, no friend more loving than Christ, our Lord. We follow the teaching of the Gospel. We counsel others: "Read the Gospel. We must go back to the Gospel." But we ourselves never read it.

You believe that you know Christ, but you know him only insofar as you know the Gospel. That, too, you believe you know because you have heard over and over again certain passages, like the wise and the foolish virgins, the talents, the salt of the earth, the treasure hidden in the field. But let anybody question a Christian on some point of Scripture and he shows at once his lack of knowledge. He does not know the text, nor its meaning, he has never reflected upon it, he has never taken the trouble to inquire about it!

Furthermore, and you know how true it is, he never speaks of it spontaneously. He has nothing to say about it. He has no desire to speak of it. The mouth speaks from the abundance of the heart. Our silence on any truly religious subject comes from our incompetence, from our lack of interest, from our coldness of heart.

But, you may say, I have tried, I began reading the Gospel but it said nothing to me. The events of Christ's life were already too familiar, all the people seemed so lifeless, the words meant nothing, so I did not bother with it any more.

What an avowal! Ought not such a reaction trouble us, stimulate us, rather than discourage us?

The word of God does not speak to us!

The word of God says nothing to us!

God speaks to us and we find it tiresome!

And all the while it is said, "My sheep hear my voice and they follow me." "He who is of God, hears the word of God." And also, "Because you are not of God you do not understand my words."

If the Gospel does not speak to you it is because you have not read it as you should. You have read it as though it were an ordinary book, looking for the subject, the plot of the story, and the conclusion.

But the Gospel is not an ordinary book. It is a sacred book, a book by which you communicate with God, as in the Eucharist. Suppose a little altar boy, wanting to know how a host tastes, should, by some accident, pick up a consecrated host. It would not be a sacrilege because the child did not know that it was consecrated, but neither would he be receiving holy communion. He supposed it to be but ordinary bread and, for him, it was no more than that. He would not receive an atom of grace. In the same way, the sacred Scripture, if it is read as though it were an ordinary book, will be for its reader an ordinary book, closed, sealed, profaned.

The Bible should be read, so to speak, on one's knees, touched with the utmost respect, opened as though one would listen, as though one would consult him who speaks.

The Fathers of the Church say that the same grace is necessary for the hearer of a prophecy as for its utterer. The purpose of Scripture is to enable us to participate in the religious experience of the inspired author. The same Spirit who breathed those words the first time must breathe them again so that they are addressed to us personally and as if they concerned ourselves above all.

80

Our Orthodox brethren do not reserve the sacred species on the altar. Rather, the place of honor is given to the sacred Scriptures, and that is quite logical. You may communicate but once a day, but you can listen to Christ as often as you wish, as often as you have need.

In the Eucharistic bread, he is present. He receives you, he listens to you.

In the Book, he speaks to you.

And who listens? Who receives his communication?

What is this respect, this attention, this faith with which we should read the Gospel?

It is something more than to believe that everything found in it is true, and actually happened. That is but the faith that you accord to any book of history. There you also believe that whatever is recorded actually took place.

The word of God is a word of revelation. You have not understood anything of sacred Scripture as long as you have not seen it applied to yourself, as long as it has not revealed you to yourself, as long as it has not become the Light of your life, a revelation of the design of God, the plan of God concerning your life. Each of us is foretold in the Gospel—seen, described, prophesied. Have you found your passage, your place, your role, the event that concerns you, the word that is addressed to you?

Even the scandal of your disgust for the word of God is foretold in Scripture. The Hebrews in the desert ended by being disgusted with the manna. They found it tasteless, insipid, monotonous, just as we find the Gospel. And they recalled the onions, the leeks, the garlic, the cucumbers of Egypt. "Here, we see nothing but that manna. . . !" If the Gospel does not taste good to you, perhaps it is because your palate is accustomed to spicier and more pungent food?

What is the Gospel?

It is God who came to live among men.

But God is always living among men. "Behold I am with you all days, even unto the consummation of the world."

God is always the same, —loving and suffering; doing good and yet unknown; just and yet persecuted.

And men are always the same, —sure of themselves, dull, unconscious, blind, heavy, hard of hearing and hard of heart.

The Gospel reveals to us that the Word was made flesh and that he came to live among us, and also how God treats men and how men treat God—maltreat him, rather.

For us also the Light shines in the darkness, the Light which enlightens every man coming into this world, and the darkness does not comprehend it. They refuse, they fear to comprehend it.

The Gospel is actual. It would not be worth a second of attention if it spoke to us of things that took place two thousand years ago. When you receive communion, you do not receive the Christ of two thousand years ago but the Christ who is living and loving you today. And when you read the Gospel it is he who is speaking to you.

Do not think that God spoke two thousand years ago and that he has been silent ever since, that we are living according to this "deposit of faith." God has no more ceased to be "revelation" than he has ceased to be Love. Whoever loves, visits the other and listens to the other. If God love you, he speaks to you.

The Holy Spirit continues to "inspire" the letter of the Scriptures. He repeats to us, he "breathes" to us all that Jesus said to his contemporaries. It is God's joy to reveal himself to us just as much today as yesterday. He does not force any one to listen to him, but no one has listened and not heard.

Do you listen to him?

The Gospel is a mirror. What does one do with a mirror? One does not use it to see the past. In a mirror one sees oneself. And what do we do?

We look at others. "How could the Jews have been so bad two thousand years ago? God was among them and they did not recognize him. They crucified him." But those Jews were not any worse than yourself. They did all that in good faith, with a good conscience. They did what they did just as we do things, without knowing what we are really doing. But we ought to know, because their example should warn us. Like them we are awaiting the Lord of glory, coming on the clouds of heaven, and he is already amongst us, at our side. We eat him in the bread, drink him in the wine, ignore him in the most insignificant of our neighbors. He is absorbed into us, nailed to us, so close to us that our glance passes over him when we look for him.

David, the most sympathetic person in the Old Testament, a hero, a poet, with a heart both delicate and enthusiastic in the service of God, allowed himself to commit a most odious crime in a moment of passion. He did it just like any one of us, smothering his conscience and endeavoring not to know. He killed the husband of a woman whom he loved and then married her.

But there was a prophet in Israel, that is, someone to whom the word of God became living, activating, unmasking. He came to find the king and said to him, "My King, may I tell you something?" "Speak," said the King. "In one of your cities there were two men, one rich and the other poor. The rich man had sheep and cattle in abundance. The poor man had only a single little sheep. He kept it in his house and it grew up with his children, eating bread with them and drinking from the same cup and sleeping at night near her master. It was like a daughter to him. A guest came to the house of the rich man, and as the rich man did not like to take a sheep from his own flock for his guest's meal, he stole the sheep of the poor man and prepared a feast."

David became angry. "That man deserves to be put to death! How could any one do such an abominable thing!"

"That man is you!" said the prophet.

And from the moment that the King regarded the words of the prophet Nathan, not as a story, a story about another, but as a revelation, a prophecy of his own deeds, his sincere, but hypocritical, indignation ceased. He saw himself in the mirror of the word of God. He knew what he had done and he repented.

The word of God has not changed. It is still living, revealing, acting.

We gather at Mass in order to assist at the recommencement, at the revival, of a few words of the Gospel. The true Gospel of the Mass is not the one that has just been read. It is the consecration. At that time a passage of the Gospel is read with faith, heard with faith, placed under the action of the same Spirit who inspired it in the past. It becomes active, it accomplishes among us that which it declares and signifies.

How active it is, that word of God!

Every day, before communion, we say—sincerely? or mechanically?—"Lord, I am not worthy that you should enter under my roof; say but the word and my soul will be healed."

And each one of us has, either with him or in his home, this Book that is filled with healing words. For what are we waiting in order to make trial of them and proof of our faith?

At the consecration, the priest pronounces a word over the bread, and the bread is cured, transformed, transubstantiated.

At the communion, we are nourished by a word from the mouth of God. Ask that you may receive it and may hear it in such a way, and with such faith, that each soul may be nourished, cured, and changed.

10.

The Sacrament
of the Church

"Outside the Church there is no salvation" (Pius IX). The first time a man of gallant soul hears this, he feels more than surprise or revolt. He suffers.

Can particularism of salvation exist? Would the love of God be considered a privilege? How can people rejoice that they alone have been saved? Would the immense majority of men who apparently do not belong to the Church be damned? Evidently not. That some poorly instructed Catholics doubt the thought of the Church and actually slant it is a scandal. God wants to save all men. He offers his grace to each and everyone. He uses the Church as a means of salvation, and not as a means of segregating some.

The Church is Catholic. Not only is she opened to all, but she is at the service of all. She prays every day "for the salvation of the whole world." She refuses to be nothing but the Church of the baptized. She is the Church of all humanity, and she saves those who do not know her but who would not refuse her if they really knew her.

Luckily, innumerable men are invisibly attached to this visible Church. All men who have not heard the Gospel preached, or all those, more numerous still, who heard it preached very poorly, whether they dwell in Kamchatka or work in a large unchristianized city, at certain moments of their life, in the secret of their heart decide for or against their conscience. If they act accordingly, they are justified. They receive grace and are incorporated to Christ.

Unwittingly and unwillingly, while they do not even dream of receiving baptism—this thought may even horrify them—they receive grace and the effect of baptism. They become members of Christ, and so, invisibly but really, members of his body, which is the Church.

The day that such a man will convert himself, that is, recognize in the Church this will of God that he was looking for and respected in his conscience, he will deny nothing which led him that far. He will only be more faithful to himself.

For us, Christians, the Church is Christ poured out and communicated. She is the permanent incarnation of God, the Savior. We should not be more offended by the adage: outside the Church there is no salvation, than we are astonished by Christ's words: "No man comes to the Father but through me" (John 14, 6).

Those who are scandalized to hear the Church vindicate the rights she holds from Christ would also have been scandalized to hear the Son of the carpenter of Nazareth say that he was the true vine and that, without him, no one could do anything. By being faithful to Christ, the Church repeats what Christ has said about himself, because she believes, with all her soul, that her only reason for being is to continue Christ. It is Christ who said, "If he refuse to hear . . . the Church, let him be to thee as the heathen and the publican" (Matthew 18, 17).

But Christ saves thousands of men who have never known him, who do not confess his name, but who act towards the least of his brethren as if they had known him. Christ judges each man according to his heart and his conscience, not according to his official belonging to a faith. The Church acts likewise: she believes that all those who in the secret of their heart open to the will of God belong to her more surely than her nominal members.

The Church is the sacrament par excellence, but God did not bind his grace exclusively to the sacraments. All have substitutions for those who can not receive them. Baptism of water may be supplemented by baptism of desire or by baptism of blood. Spiritual communion may replace real communion. The act of perfect contrition restores the state of grace as confession does. In certain circumstances, you may marry validly without the presence of a priest. Thus, belonging to the Church may be the result of a desire that does not express itself in a rite. Moreover, that desire may be implicit. As all those who wish to obey God, who is Christ, are attached to the Church, so all those who want to obey their conscience are attached to the Church. No man of good faith is excluded from the Church or from salvation. The light shines on every man who comes into this world, and to remain in darkness, one must have voluntarily sinned against light.

But Christ demands that all these invisible members enter the paternal house, eat the children's bread, and become visible members of his body. He who came to reassemble the children of God who are scattered, he who desired that there would be but one flock and one shepherd, he made us responsible for this great gathering of his sheep. We Christians are, towards each other, as elder sons who enjoy their privileges instead of sharing with younger or with retarded children. We are like wealthy nations

91

who refuse assistance to underdeveloped countries. Numerous are the nations that are spiritually underdeveloped. Numerous are the nations that have not yet known the Church, or worse still, who have known her without recognizing her, because we have deformed her, bound her to political and social forms that are contingent and positively unjust; so much so, that it is their conscience, their probity, their sense of justice and truth that led them to reject the Church. Through our faults, invisible to the eyes of too many people, we maintain a Church that Christ would have wanted so beautiful and so united, that all, seeing her, may know that the Father has sent him.

Outside the Church there is no salvation. And what about within the Church? The more we have received, the more will be exacted of us. This adage, which seems at first sight to re-assure us of our privileges, should disturb us as it makes us conscious of our responsibilities. We must not evangelize the pagans so that they may be saved more easily. To become a Christian increases the burden of our responsibilities since each is judged according to the talents he has received. Christianity is first of all a means of loving God and not a dispensation from effort or an assurance of salvation.

It will not be the pagans who will be lost without us. God will save them if they are of good will, but we are lost without them because we shall not have performed our duty.